WEIRDO 7

MEGA WEIRD!

Scholastic Press
An imprint of Scholastic Australia Pty Limited (ABN 11 000 614 577)
PO Box 579 Gosford NSW 2250
www.scholastic.com.au

Part of the Scholastic Group
Sydney • Auckland • New York • Toronto • London • Mexico City
• New Delhi • Hong Kong • Buenos Aires • Puerto Rico

A catalogue record for this book is available from the National Library of Australia

ISBN : 978-93-5471-863-2

Typeset in Grenadine MVB, Push Ups and Lunch Box.

This reprint edition, November 2024

Printed in India at Polykam Offset New Delhi 110028

ANH DO

Illustrated by JULES FABER

WEIRDO 7

MEGA WEIRD!

A SCHOLASTIC PRESS BOOK
FROM SCHOLASTIC AUSTRALIA

MEGA
BUCKS!

CHAPTER 1

People usually put **cars** in garages, don't they?

Well, **not us!**

WHEEEEEE
EEEEEE
EEEEEE
EEEEEEEE!

We have everything **BUT** the car in our garage! It's **so full of stuff**, we have to keep our car **on the street**.

Guess

which one

it is . . .

It's actually **really** cool that we have so much stuff in our garage . . . because the **MEGA STREET GARAGE SALE** is coming up and Mum says it's our chance to turn **ALL** of our junk into **MEGA BUCKS!**

ONE MILLION DOLLARS.
I'LL TAKE IT!

Imagine what sort of bike I could get for one **million bucks**? It would be the **FERRARI** of bikes!

On Sunday, **everyone** in our street will join in.

MEGA

STREET SALE

This Sunday!

Pick up a bargain!

People come from **all over town** to check it out!

Hopefully someone will come looking for this **headless ninja hamster**.

Mum and Dad think **everything's** worth selling.

Granddad thinks so, too.

Hmm, maybe a school of **really old** sharks could use them . . .

'Someone could use this,' said Dad, pulling out an **old rocking chair.**

'But I'm pretty sure it still works,' he said, before sitting on it.

I thought the seat of the chair might **rip** . . .

Or that the legs would **collapse** ...

I did **not** expect Dad to go ...

WHOOOAAAAAA

AHHHHHHHHHH!

DOES THIS THING

HAVE ANY BRAKES?!

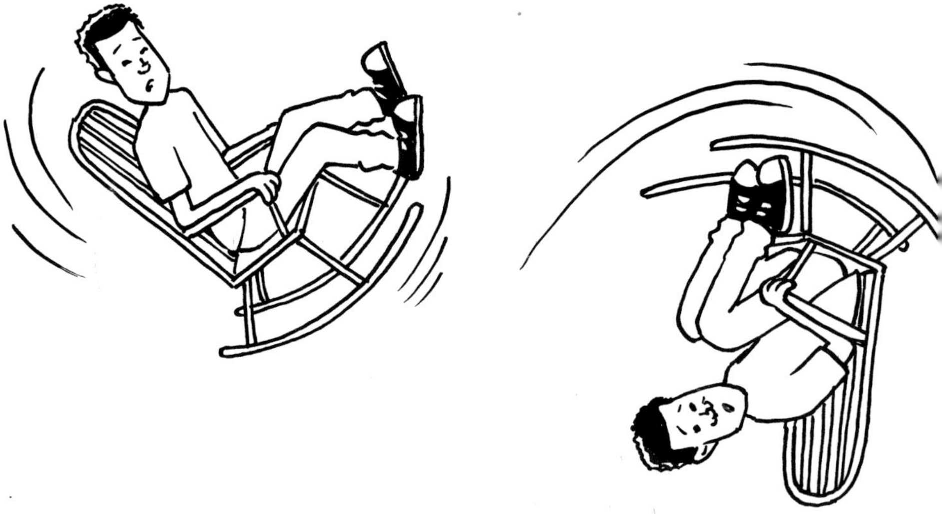

...**rolling** down the road!

I FOUND A LOLLIPOP!

Our pile of stuff is **ENORMOUS**.

It's going to take ages to sort through it all.

It's as big as **Mount Everest**!

Me and Sally keep thinking about what we could do with all the **money** we're going to make!

'What if we got **a pool?**' I said.

'Great idea!' said Sally. 'A **really big one** with a **slippery-dip!**'

'**Yeah!** And what if we had **waterslides** attached to our bedroom windows?' I said. 'Then we could just jump right in!'

SPLASH!
SPLASH!

AWESOME!

'Or what about a **treehouse?**' I said.

Bella and Henry could get one too, and we could connect them down the street with **bridges**!

HENRY,
HENRY,
HENRY!

MEET ME
ON THE
BRIDGE
AFTER DINNER?

I'LL BE THERE!

FiDo and Blockhead barked, as if to say **'What about something for us?'**

'We won't forget you guys,' said Sally. 'How about we buy you two some **singing lessons?**'

A-WOOOOOOOOOOOOOOOOOOOOOOOOOOOOOOOOOOOOOOOOOOOOOOOOOOOOOOOOOOOO!

'What do **you** want us to buy, Roger?' I asked my brother.

Roger wanted **dirt**?

Mum and Dad appeared from behind some junk, covered in **dust** and **cobwebs**.

KIDS,

YOUR DAD AND I ALREADY HAVE A PLAN FOR THE MONEY...

Me and Sally frowned at each other.

Mum and Dad probably wanted to buy a **new can opener** or a **broom** or . . .

something

REALLY,

REALLY

BORING.

'We're going to buy everyone **brand new undies!**' said Dad.

UNDIES?!
UNDIES . . .
YES!

'Just kidding!' said Dad.

WE'RE GOING TO FLY
GRANDMA DO
OVER FROM VIETNAM!

What? Grandma Do!? We hadn't seen her in **aaaaages!**

Grandma Do is the **best!** She's so **funny** and **cool**. We always have so much fun together!

This was **THE GREATEST NEWS ever!**

Now we **really** had to make sure we could make enough money from the garage sale!

JUNK PILE!

CHAPTER 2

By the end of the day, we'd almost made it to the bottom of the **junk pile**.

We'd sorted everything into smaller piles.

Old . . .

Really old . . .

And stuff that was **so old**,
even **cavemen** would think so.

Problem was, Mum and Dad kept finding things they wanted to **keep** . . .

Dad kept digging up **falling-apart clothes**.

Or clothes that wouldn't fit **anyone!**

'I don't think so, Dad,' I said.

And Mum kept finding things that she figured she could, 'use for something.'

'What if I turned this **broken umbrella** into a **rain hat**?'

'Or my **old bike** into a **unicycle**?'

'Or these old mop heads into a pair of Slide and Shine Shoes?'

Slide and Shine Shoes?

Mum and Dad were **forgetting** why we were doing this!

'Mum, Dad . . .' I said. 'We need to make money for **Grandma Do's visit**, remember?'

'You're right, Weir,' said Mum. 'I'll get to work on fixing a few things **for the sale**.'

'Me too,' said Dad.

'Don't look at me,' said Sally. 'I wouldn't have a clue.'

'Me neither,' I said.

BUT I KNOW SOMEONE WHO HAS A SEWING MACHINE!

THE WEIRDEST!

CHAPTER 3

Everyone on our street was getting ready for the **SALE**. People had bits and pieces

everywhere!

Mr McDool was selling the **biggest** collection of **Sparkly Pony Dolls** I'd ever seen.

My neighbours Will and Hugh were selling some of their **trucks**.

Hans Some was selling his collection of **mirrors**.

No-one had as much stuff as **us**, though!

When I reached Bella's house, I got a big surprise. Her family's garage was completely . . .

EMPTY.

'Hi Weir,' said Bella. She was sitting on the front steps, writing on a **notepad**.

'Hey Bella,' I said. 'Your garage is so **neat**. You should see ours. We've been sorting for hours, but you **still can't see the floor!**'

Bella looked up.

'Someone snuck into our garage the other day and took what we had . . . The worst thing is, they **took my mum's sewing machine**,' she said.

That was **terrible**. Was this one of those times where I was supposed to give her a **hug**?

I'm not really the **huggy type** . . .

'Weir, what are you doing?' said Bella, looking up at me weirdly.

What **was** I doing?

UMM . . .
JUST.
BEING. A.
ROBOT . . .
TO . . .
MAKE.
YOU.
LAUGH.

Bella laughed.

It worked!

YOU'RE WEIRD,
WEIR DO.
HAHAHA.

I didn't want to tell Bella that I was hoping we could borrow her sewing machine . . .

'I'm just getting a **sneak peek** at what everyone has for the **STREET SALE**. We are hoping to make enough money to get **Grandma over from Vietnam**.'

'Cool!' said Bella. 'Is she as **weird** as you guys?'

Grandma Do loves to **play pranks**.

'The last time we visited her, she **jumped** out the front door **dressed like a gorilla!**'

'Then there was this other time when we were in the **middle of a picnic**, wondering where Grandma had gone . . .'

WHERE'S
GRANDMA?

'Then she **jumped** out of a tree and landed on our lunch!'

We just hope Grandma never wears the **gorilla suit** to the zoo, just in case they think she's a **real gorilla**.

'What are you writing?' I asked Bella.

'Have you heard about the **school writing competition?**' she said. 'There's **prize money** for first place.

You can write **ANYTHING** you want. A story, a poem . . . anything. I'm trying to write a **winning song**,' said Bella, 'so I can get my mum a new sewing machine. Got any tips?'

'I think you should write about something you **really love** . . .' I said. 'Like **animals**.'

GREAT IDEA, WEIR!

TA-DA!

CHAPTER 4

Without a sewing machine, Dad picked up his **old clothes** and gave the **needle and thread** a go.

Turns out he is **REALLY BAD** at sewing!

ADD ANOTHER FIVE LEGS AND I'D BUY THEM!

Meanwhile, I had just **one corner** of the garage left to sort through.

HUGE pile of stuff!

UGH . . .

At the very bottom of the pile was something really **big** and **heavy**, wrapped in an old blanket . . .

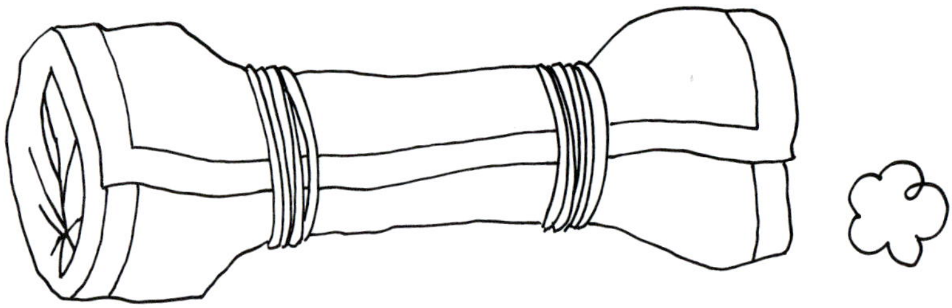

What was it?

When I pulled the blanket off, there was a **MASSIVE** cloud of dust.

And once it all settled and I could see again . . .

I saw **the most amazing** thing . . .

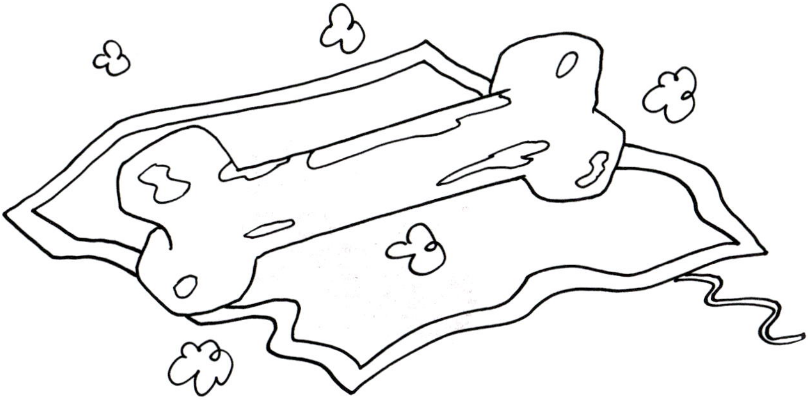

Wow!

DINO
BONE?

CHAPTER 5

Dad helped me get **the bone** over to Henry's house.

We thought Henry's dad might be able to help us figure out **exactly** what it was we'd found in our garage.

'Well, I'm no expert in **fossils**,' he said, 'but I think you have yourself a **dinosaur bone**.'

'Where did it come from?' Mr O'Henry asked.

Dad explained how a **funny old uncle** of his had given it to him years ago.

'But he also gave me a button he said was a **time machine** and a cleaning brush he said would **make your hair grow** . . . so I didn't think much of it!'

BRUSH YOUR SCALP WITH THIS AND YOUR HAIR WILL GROW BACK!

AND THIS ONE HERE'S A DINO BONE!
HA! A DINO BONE, SURE THING, UNCLE.

'I had no idea it really **could** have been a **dino bone!**' said Dad.

'Well, I don't know for sure,' said Mr O'Henry, 'but I'll take it to the **museum** tomorrow and have an **expert** look at it.'

'Wow!' said Henry. 'I wonder what **dinosaur** it belonged to!'

'Or what about a **P-terodactyl?**' I suggested.

'It's said like **Ter-o-dactyl**,' explained Dad, like the word began with a **'t'** not a **'p'**.

That made me think up a **great joke**.

WHY CAN'T YOU HEAR A PTERODACTYL IN THE LOO?

WHY?

BECAUSE THE 'P' IS SILENT!

HA HA
HA HA HA
HA HA HA HA

DEAL?

CHAPTER 6

The street was **packed** with people on the

MEGA GARAGE SALE DAY!

Mum and Dad were doing their best to **be funny** so that people would come and take a look at our stuff.

WE'VE GOT POTS,
WE'VE GOT PANS!

WE'VE GOT HEATERS,
WE'VE GOT FANS!

READ THEM IN BED, OR PUT THEM ON YOUR HEAD!

At least they were making **us** laugh . . .

Even Roger, FiDo and Blockhead did their best to help sell things.

Everyone **loved** the show,

but they **didn't buy much** from us . . .

ONE MILLION DOLLARS.
I'LL GIVE YOU ONE DOLLAR.
DEAL.

There were **some surprises** . . .

But aside from a few
other bits and pieces . . .

and . . .

. . . we didn't really sell that much.

Definitely not enough to get **Grandma Do** over for a visit . . .

So much for

MEGA BUCKS!

Maybe I needed to enter the **writing competition** too . . .

We all wanted to see Grandma Do **so** badly. That **prize money** would **really** help.

BELCH-
MAN!

CHAPTER 7

On the bus to school, **Bella** was still **scribbling** in her notepad.

'Almost,' said Bella.

'I bet it's great,' I said. 'I'm going to enter the competition too,' I told Bella, and showed her a bunch of **dinosaur jokes** I'd written.

Whenever Bella says something nice to me, I **blush**. It's a bit **embarrassing**.

Sometimes I wish I could wear **clown make-up** all the time and then no-one could tell when I was **red in the face**.

'Hey, Weir, can you **help** me finish my song today?' said Bella.

'Of course!'

Bella and I spent **all of recess** working on her song. It was **so much fun!**

It turns out . . .

I'M PRETTY GOOD AT
RHYMING WORDS . . .
ANIMALS, FISH AND EVEN BIRDS!
I NEVER KNEW I HAD THIS SKILL,
BUT IT GIVES ME
QUITE A THRILL!

By the time we finished the song,
it was **awesome**.

YES!

Bella was in with a **real** shot!

We **both** were!

We handed in our entries and wished each other luck.

'Good luck to you, **too**,' I said. 'That's a great song, you know it's **true**.'

'Are you still rhyming?' asked Bella.

'I'd like to say I've given it the **chop**, but it's really, **really** hard to **stop**.'

Quite a few kids had entered the comp and we were all **really excited** to find out who'd won!

Blake Green had written a **poem** about how lonely it is being the **school bully**. He read some to us at lunch.

OH, HOW MUCH I YEARN,
TO BE KNOWN FOR MORE
THAN GIVING ARM-BURNS.
WHY DO I MAKE THE
OTHER KIDS EDGY?
MAYBE I SHOULD STOP
GIVING THEM
WEDGIES?

Henry had written a **story** about a **superhero** who could fight crime by **burping**.

'And the city was safe,' said Henry, 'thanks to Belchman.'

At the end of the day, we had a **special** assembly to announce the **winner**. The judges—Miss Franklin and Mr Bongo—were going to pick their **favourite entry**.

'It was a **very close competition**,' said Mr Bongo. 'We had so many **brilliant** entries. But two **REALLY stood out**. They were both very clever and very funny!'

'We can only have **ONE** winner . . . but Miss Franklin and I can't decide! So if you hear your name,' said Mr Bongo, 'could you please come up on stage?'

BELLA ALLEN . . .
AND
WEIR DO!

We were the **top two!**

Bella and I turned and high-fived each other, then we walked up to the stage together.

I **really** wanted to win so that I could pay for Grandma's flights . . . but I also wanted Bella to win so that she could replace her mum's **sewing machine**. I didn't know **WHAT** I wanted!

'We're going to need **EVERYONE'S** help to decide the winner!' said Miss Franklin.

Bella and I had to read what we'd written, then whoever had the **loudest cheers** from the crowd would take out the **top prize!**

I was up first!

I held my collection of jokes and started reading them out.

What do you call a dinosaur that's just run a marathon?

My-feet-are-sore-us.

Why do so many dinosaurs have such long necks?

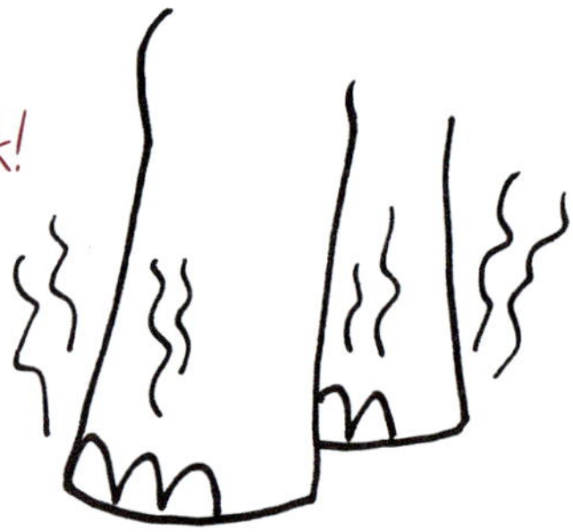

Because their feet stink!

What do you get if you cross a kangaroo with a Triceratops?

A Tricera-hops!

What do you call a dinosaur that stomps on everything?

Tyrannosaurus Wrecks!

What do you call a dinosaur with a guitar?

Tyrannosaurus Rocks!

Everyone was **laughing**!

My jokes were a **hit**! They were laughing so much—**it felt great!**

Once the laughter settled down, it was Bella's turn. She smiled at me and I handed her the mic.

Then Bella began to sing her song.

WHAT DO THEY DO WITH ALL THE POO
FROM ALL THE ANIMALS AT THE ZOO?
THE HIPPOS,
THE TIGERS, THE KANGAROOS—
WHAT DO THEY DO WITH
ALL THAT POO?
I WONDER,
DON'T YOU
WONDER, TOO?

WELL, MY BROTHER TOLD ME
THE OTHER DAY,
THAT BIG TRUCKS COME
AND TAKE IT AWAY.
AND THEY MIX IT WITH ALL KINDS
OF MATERIAL . . .
AND MAKE IT INTO
CHILDREN'S
BREAKFAST
CEREAL.

The crowd was **LOVING** it! They were all **laughing** and **clapping!**

Bella grinned and kept going . . .

BUT MY SISTER SAID
THAT'S NOT RIGHT,
SHE SAID THAT THEY PICK IT ALL
UP AT NIGHT.
AND THEY MIX IT ALL IN A
BIG MACHINE . . .
AND MAKE IT INTO
CHOCOLATE
ICE-CREAM.

HA HA HA
HA HA HA
HA HA HA
HA HA HA
HA HA HA

I SAY,
WHAT DO THEY DO
WITH ALL THE POO
FROM ALL THE ANIMALS
AT THE ZOO?
I WONDER,
DON'T YOU
WONDER, TOO?

The crowd went **nuts** and it was clear there was a **first prize winner** ...

AND FIRST PRIZE GOES TO . . .

BELLA ALLEN!

GRANDMA DO!

CHAPTER 8

Bella's mum was so happy with her **new** sewing machine.

And I was so happy Bella's song won the comp. She deserved it. Her song was **SO** funny.

I didn't take home the **prize money** ... but it didn't matter in the end!

Because we had the most **awesome** news from Mr O'Henry!

It turns out the **old bone** we found in the garage actually belonged . . . to a **T-Rex**!

Can you believe it?

'A TYRANNOSAURUS REX!'

Dad decided to give the **bone** to the local **museum**, and in return they gave us **MORE** than enough money to get **Grandma Do** over!

Mum and Dad bought us some **cool presents**, too, for our hard work at the garage sale.

They took me and Sally to

WILD WATER ADVENTURE PARK!

OHOOOOOOOOOO
OOOOOOOOOOOO
OOOOOOOOOOOO
OOOOOOOOOOOO
OOOOOOOOOOOO

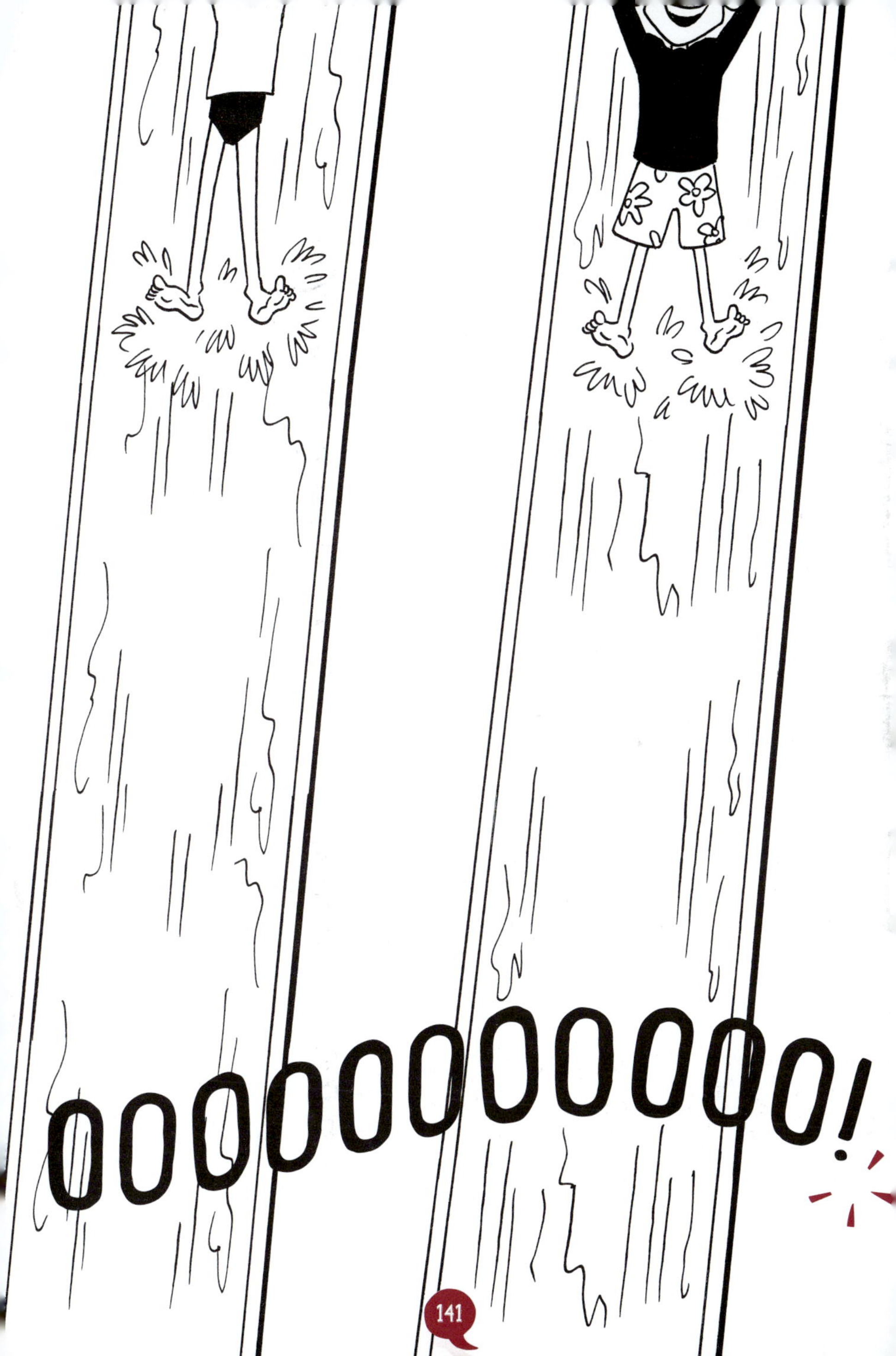
OOOOOOOOOOO!

SPLA

SH!

WHERE'D MY PANTS GO?!

They gave FiDo and Blockhead
a **karaoke singing machine**.

They gave Granddad a **new container** for his teeth . . .

And they gave Roger . . .

A worm farm! Filled with dirt!

EAT?
EEK!
NO!

So what about **Grandma Do**?

Well, she'll be **on her way over** to see us real soon! **We can't wait!**

Neither can Grandma!

Let the pranks begin!

FROM ANH

For **Suzie**,

who beat me at Scrabble.

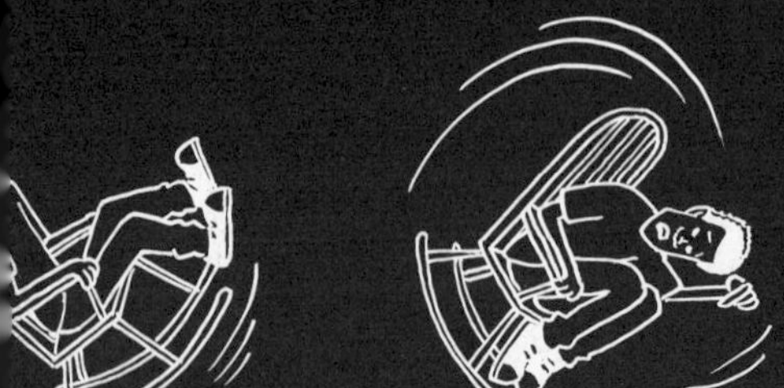

ACKNOWLEDGEMENTS

FROM JULES

For **Bec** and **Dax** and
Willow and **Ryder**
because I always said
Book 7 could be yours.

AUSTRALIAN BOOK INDUSTRY AWARDS WINNER!

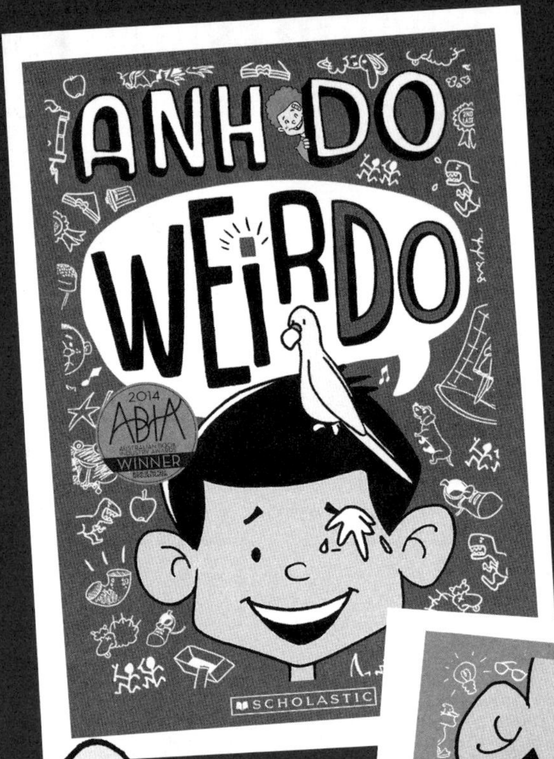

Book 1

GOT IT!

bird

Book 2

GOT IT!

COLLECT THEM ALL!

Book 3

GOT IT!

Book 4

GOT IT!

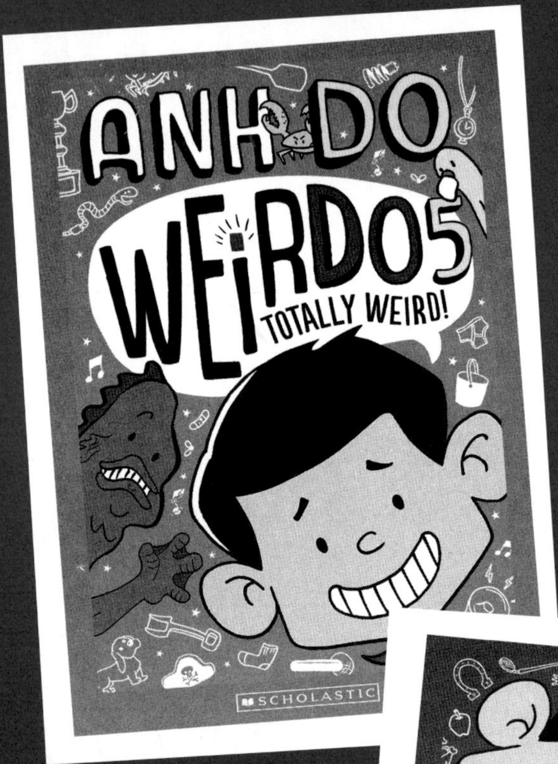

Book 5

GOT IT!

Book 6

GOT IT!

COLLECT THEM ALL!
YOU CAN NEVER HAVE TOO MANY WEIRDOS
ANH DO
WEIRDO 7
MEGA WEIRD!
SCHOLASTIC
ladybug!
Book 7
GOT IT!
gnomes
dino bone!

STAY TUNED!